Primary concerns

**Dave Boyle
Wendy Pitt**

CAMBRIDGE UNIVERSITY PRESS

Published by the Press Syndicate of the University of Cambridge
The Pitt Building, Trumpington Street, Cambridge CB2 1RP
40 West 20th Street, New York, NY 10011–4211, USA
10 Stamford Road, Oakleigh, Victoria 3166, Australia

In association with Staffordshire County Council

© Cambridge University Press 1992

First published 1992

Printed in Great Britain by Scotprint Limited, Musselburgh

Designed and Produced by Gecko Limited, Bicester, Oxon.

A catalogue record for this book is available from the British Library.

ISBN 0 521 40626 9

PICTURE ACKNOWLEDGEMENTS

Bate Collection of Musical Instruments, Oxford 29tr, 29c.
Jonathan Cape Ltd. (Roald Dahl, *The Minipins*) 5tl.
Christopher Coggins 11, 12, 25ct, 26, 28t, 28b, 29bl.
Glory Farm County Primary School, Bicester 11, 28, 29bl.
Graham Portlock 32.
Robert Harding Picture Library 4t, 4c, 4b, 14b, 15cl, 15bl, 21, 25tr, 29br, 30t.
Rob Judges 18, 19c, 22, 24cb, 24b, 25cl, 25c, 25br, 27, 29tr, 29c, 30cb.
Lego U.K. Ltd. 5bl.
Philips Electronic and Associated Industries Ltd. 19t.
Linda Proud 14t.
Redferns 25cr, 25bl.
Reebok Ltd. 5br.
Walls-Birdseye Ltd. 5tr.
West Oxford Primary School 18, 19c.
Zefa Ltd. 15tl, 15tr, 15br, 24t, 24ct, 25tl, 30ct, 30b.

Picture Research by Linda Proud

NOTICE TO TEACHERS

The contents of this book are in the copyright of Cambridge University Press. Unauthorised copying of any of the pages is not only illegal but also goes against the interests of the authors.

For authorised copying please check that your school has a licence (through the Local Education Authority) from the Copyright Licensing Agency which enables you to copy small parts of the text in limited numbers.

Contents

Advertising   4

On the road   14

In tune   24

Advertising

Talking together

What is advertising?
Who uses it? Why?
Do you think advertising works? How could you find out?

How many different forms of advertising can you think of?
Which adverts do you like?
Which are your favourites? Why?
Which adverts don't you like? Why?

Are adverts always accurate? Can you think of any adverts that are not?

> Make a collage showing the different forms of advertising. Don't forget papers, magazines, posters, packaging, logos, free gifts, competitions, television and radio

Roald Dahl
The Master Storyteller

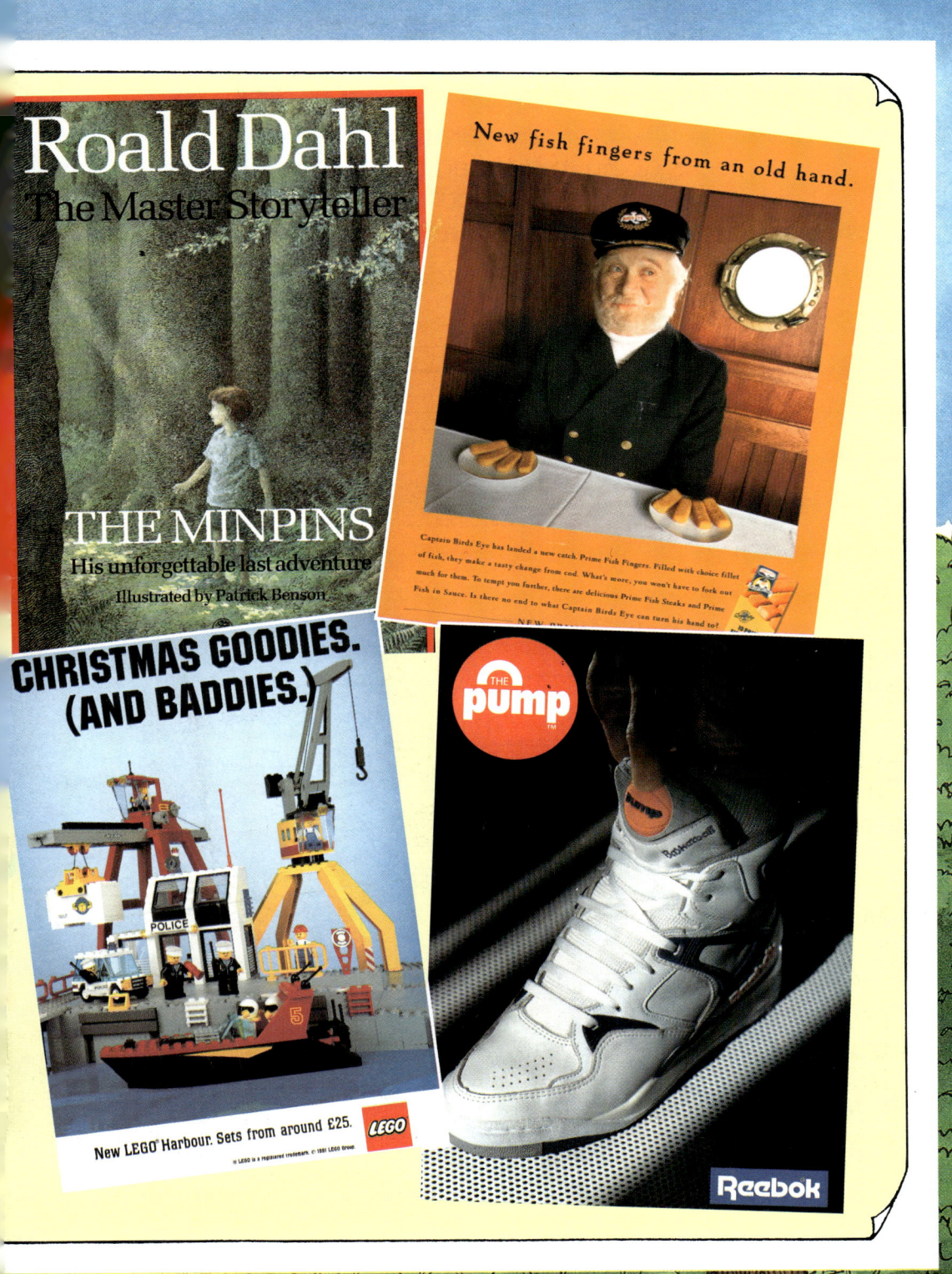

THE MINPINS
His unforgettable last adventure

Illustrated by Patrick Benson

New fish fingers from an old hand.

Captain Birds Eye has landed a new catch. Prime Fish Fingers. Filled with choice fillet of fish, they make a tasty change from cod. What's more, you won't have to fork out much for them. To tempt you further, there are delicious Prime Fish Steaks and Prime Fish in Sauce. Is there no end to what Captain Birds Eye can turn his hand to?

CHRISTMAS GOODIES.
(AND BADDIES.)

New LEGO® Harbour. Sets from around £25.

LEGO

THE pump™

Reebok

The need

A school play is planned for next term and any money raised is going to be used to help buy a new minibus. You have to make sure the children, parents, teachers and governors come to the play.

• DATA FILE •
Research:
data collection and display
Presentation

Developing your design

Planning your work

What form of advertising will be most suitable? Design a questionnaire to find out which types of adverts people like the most and display your results.

What are your favourite adverts?

Posters	Free samples	T Shirts	Leaflets	TV	Badges
✓✓✓ ✓✓	✓✓ ✓✓	✓✓	✓	✓✓✓ ✓✓✓ ✓✓	✓✓✓ ✓✓ ✓✓

What type of adverts do you like the most?

	Funny adverts	Adverts with animals	Exciting adverts	Advert you have to think about
Class 1	||||| ||||| |||||	||||| |||||		|||||
Class 2	||||| |||||	|||||	|||	||||| |||
Class 3	||||| ||||| ||||| |||	|||||	|||||	

7

Make a list of advertising slogans used in newspapers, magazines and on television. Do they have anything in common? Will you need to have an advertising slogan?

Will you need to make posters for your slogan? If so, what sort of lettering will you use?

A Mars A DAY HELPS YOU WORK REST AND PLAY

PEPSI IT'S THE TASTE

HAVE A BREAK - HAVE A KitKat

IRN-BRU MADE IN SCOTLAND FROM GIRDERS

TRANSFORMERS ROBOTS IN DISGUISE

DO YOU LOVE ANYONE ENOUGH TO GIVE THEM YOUR LAST ROLO?

POLO THE MINT WITH THE HOLE

diet Coke YOU CAN'T BEAT THE FEELING

Opal Fruits MADE TO MAKE YOUR MOUTH WATER

BEANZ MEANZ HEINZ

If you have a video camera you could plan and record an advert. What needs to be said and who will say it? Do you need props and costumes? What will happen?

- DATA FILE -
Audio/visual:
using a video camera

ideas for lettering

Practise your lettering like this

BREAKAWAY

You can cut out letters and pictures from newspapers or magazines to use.

• DATA FILE •
Graphics:
lettering 1
lettering 2

Planning a video

Design a storyboard showing each scene in your advert.

'STEP PRODUCTIONS'

Scene 1

New Minibus

Scene 2

Child explaining how money is being raised

Scene 3

Children saying why a minibus is needed

Scene 4

NAME....................
YOU ARE INVITED TO A FUND RAISING DRAMA PRODUCTION

Invitation to come to a fund raising drama production

You may want to write a script which the actors should learn before you record.

• DATA FILE •
Script writing
Story boards

More ideas

Design a poster to advertise your favourite product.

Design a new school logo.

Design and print a school sweatshirt or some headed writing paper with the new logo.

Plan and record a cassette tape which could be broadcast on local radio to advertise a special occasion at your school.

Design and make a new package to protect and advertise your favourite breakfast cereal.

12

Plan a competition which could be used to advertise a new product.

Compose a jingle which would help to sell
- a new snack
- new clothes
- a new range of sports wear

Ask a local business or industry how they advertise their products. Does this work? Could you help them? How could they help the school?

on the road

Talking together

What different types of road are there?
Who uses roads? Why?

What different sorts of vehicles are used?

What ways of communicating are used on the road?
What information needs to be communicated?
Why is this important?

Do any road users require special consideration?

What do the different road signs and markings mean?
Why are different shapes and colours used?
Where are lights used?
Where is sound used?

14

15

The need

Parents are causing a few problems with their driving and careless parking outside the school gates. They are causing a danger to children and other road users. How could you improve the traffic problem around the school? Could you devise a better system for parking?

Developing your design

What causes the problem?

How many children are collected by car?
How many children walk home?
How many children use a bicycle to get home?

What are the main difficulties at hometime?
Are there problems at any other times of the day?

	How do you get home from school?			
	Car	Bus	Bicycle	Walk
Class 1	|||| |||| |||| |||	|||		||||
Class 2	|||| |||| |||| |||			|||| |||
Class 3	||||	||||			|||| |||
Class 4	||||	|||| ||||	|||	|||| ||||

How will you collect this information?
You could
- look at school records
- conduct a survey
- design questionnaires
- interview local residents

• D A T A   F I L E •
Research:
data collection and display

17

Presenting your information

How could this information be shown to the school governors, parents or teachers? Would anyone else be interested in seeing your information?

You could use
- graphs
- models
- a computer database
- an audio tape
- a video
- photographs

• DATA FILE •

Audio/visual:
using a camera
using a tape recorder
using a video camera
Graphics
presenting work
Preparation:
myself
Presentation:
advertising methods
displaying 3D work

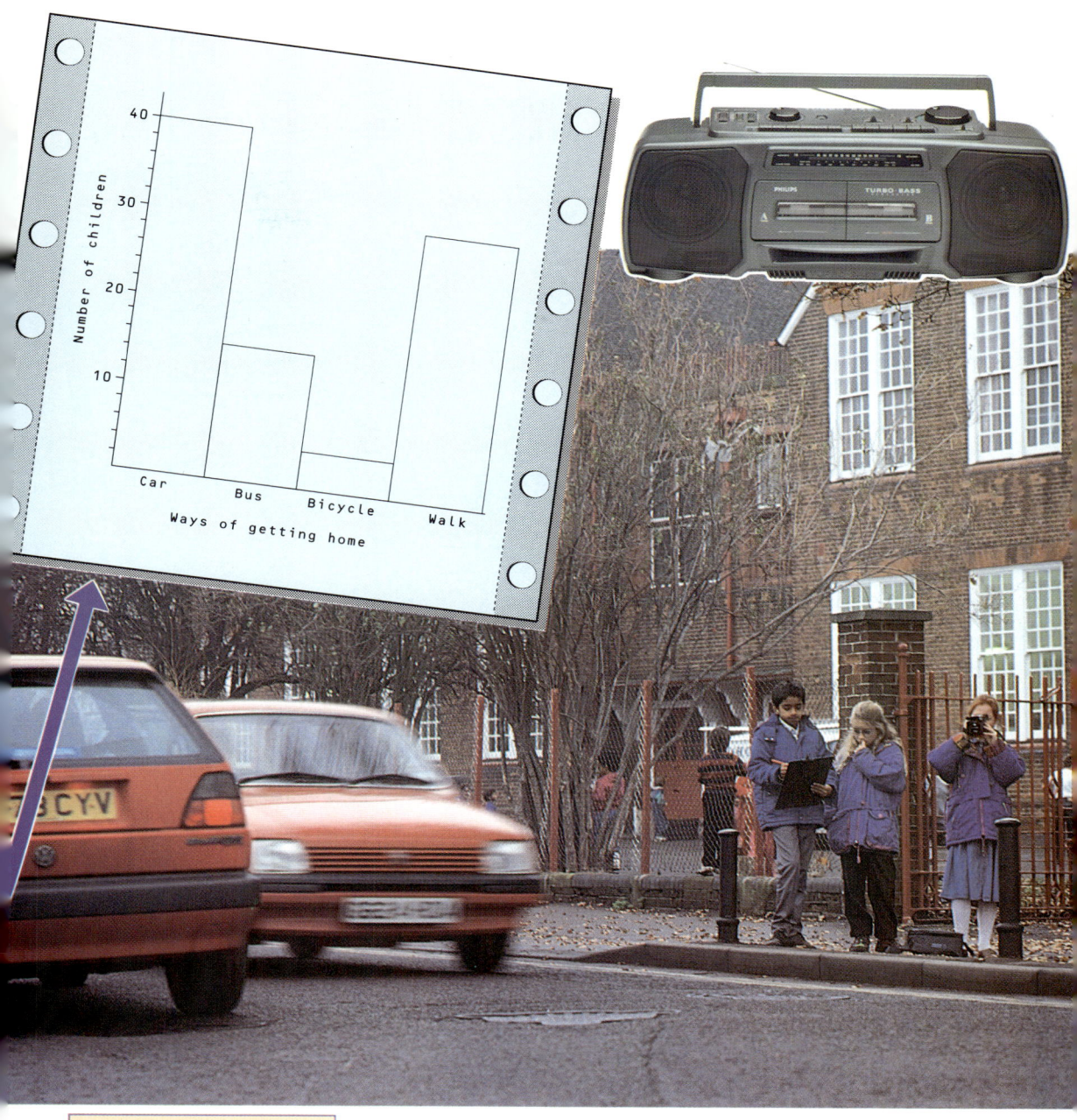

Taking action

After your enquiry, what action could be taken by
- your class
- the school
- parents
- the school governors
- the local council

19

You will need to make some proposals to show what needs to be done. How will you present your ideas?

Presenting your ideas

Make a map of the school to show how the playground and local roads could be improved.

• D A T A F I L E •

Graphics:
mapping 1
mapping 2
Printing:
on paper and card
Systems

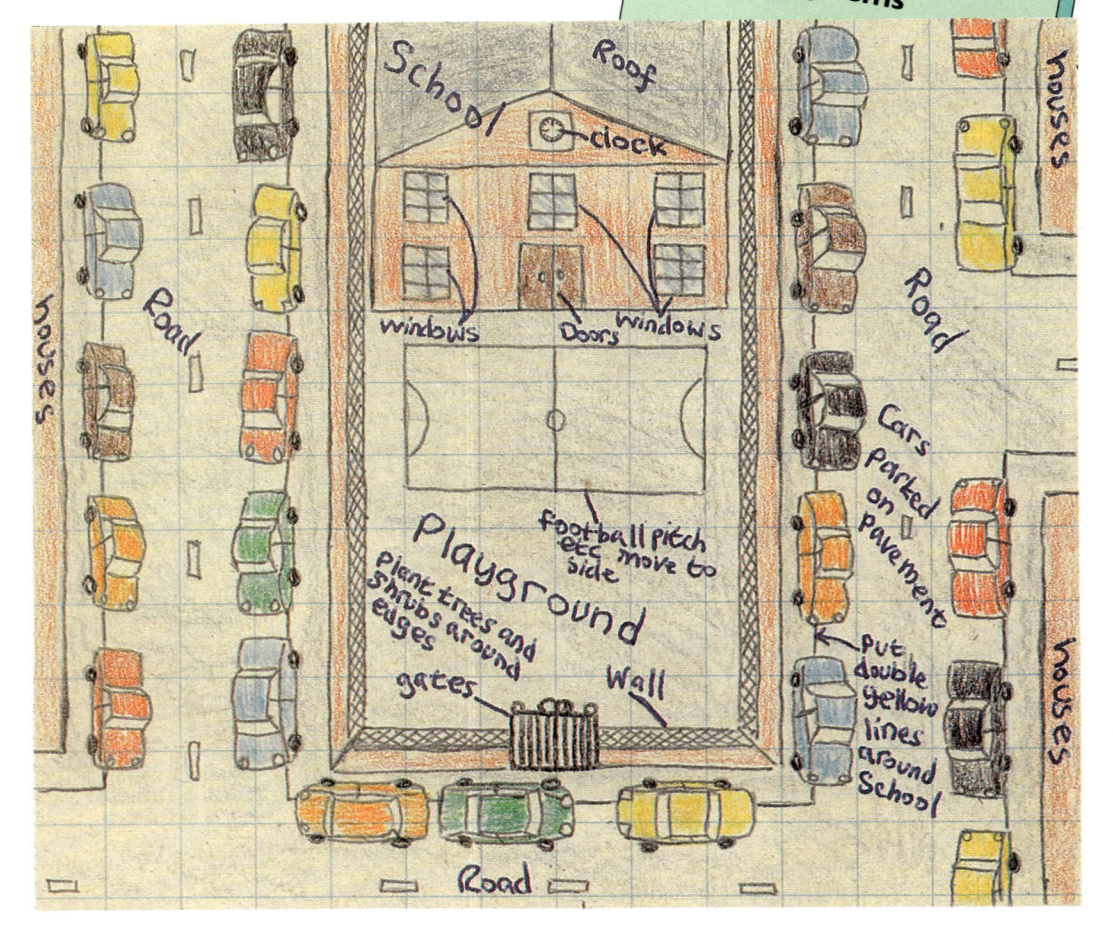

Make a model that illustrates your suggestions.

20

Design and make some new signs to be used around the school.

NO PARKING

SLOW

Devise a new system to ease the congestion at home time.

More ideas

Design and make a working set of traffic lights. You could control these by computer.
Design and make some special clothing to be worn by pedestrians or cyclists at night.

Design a system which could be used to warn other road users when a heavy vehicle is being reversed.

Design some new hazard warning signs for use on the road or on vehicles carrying dangerous loads.

Write and present a play to improve road safety.

in tune

Talking together

How many different musical instruments can you think of? How are they different? How are they the same?
How could you put them into groups? Are there any other ways of grouping them?

How many different ways of making sounds can you think of?
Do the different ways have anything in common?
How would you describe the different sounds that are made?

Which different sounds make us feel happy, sad, frightened or excited?
When is music used to change our moods and feelings?

Which is your favourite musical instrument? Why?

Make a musical display

24

25

The need

Your class is putting on an assembly for the rest of the school which includes music and sound effects. You need to design and make some musical instruments to use during the assembly.

Developing your design

Planning your work

What will the assembly be about?
Which moods and feelings are you hoping to create?
What sort of sounds will you need to make?
What special sound effects do you need?
How will you make them?

Ideas for making sounds

Look at some musical instruments to find out how they are made and how they make their sounds.

Which materials will you need to make similar instruments or new designs that will make the sounds you want?

Will they make one sound or a range of sounds?

How could the materials be joined together?

How will you make them look good?

• DATA FILE •
Sounds:
shaking, scrapping and hitting
plucking and blowing
Recycling materials

Rubbing

Rub a piece of dowel over a ribbed plastic bottle. Try rubbing at different speeds or try different bottles.

Try rubbing other things.

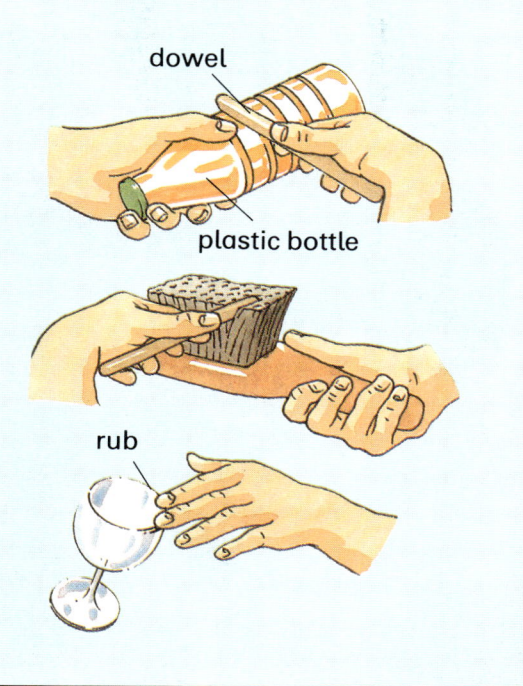

Hitting

drum
nails
water

• DATA FILE •

Sounds:
shaking, scrapping and hitting
plucking and blowing

Plucking

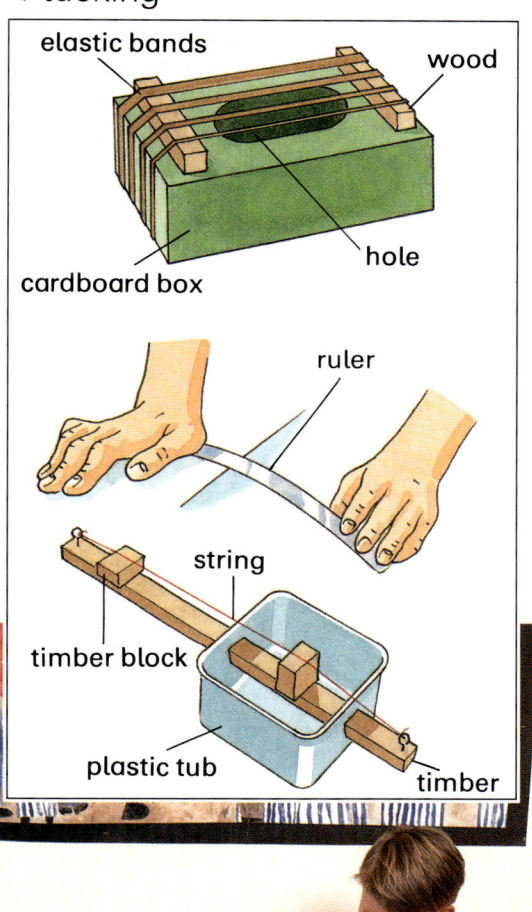

- elastic bands
- wood
- cardboard box
- hole
- ruler
- string
- timber block
- plastic tub
- timber

Blowing

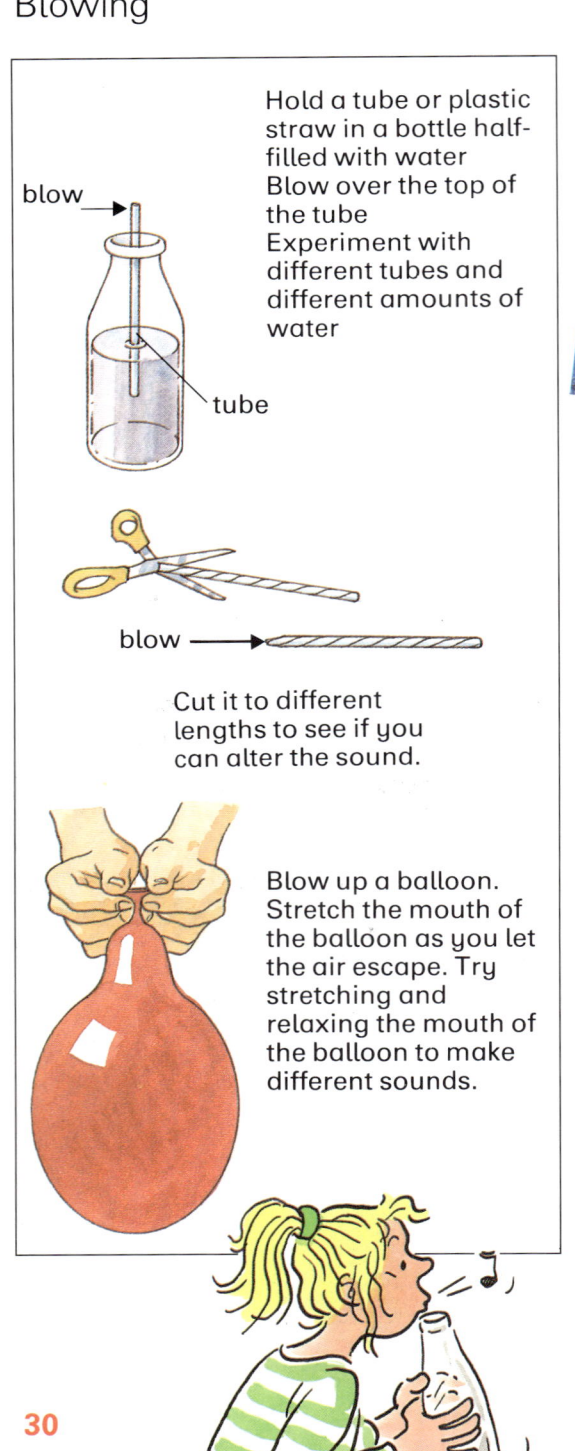

Hold a tube or plastic straw in a bottle half-filled with water. Blow over the top of the tube. Experiment with different tubes and different amounts of water.

blow

tube

blow

Cut it to different lengths to see if you can alter the sound.

Blow up a balloon. Stretch the mouth of the balloon as you let the air escape. Try stretching and relaxing the mouth of the balloon to make different sounds.

More ideas

Make some sound effects for
- a storm

- a celebration
- a sad event

- a spooky story

Devise a story for younger children with sound effects.

Make a recording of percussion rhythms for younger children to copy.

31

Compose a new advertising jingle for your favourite food.

Collect adverts from magazines and choose suitable background music for them.

Design some symbols to stand for different sounds. Put them together to represent a piece of music.

Make a recording of percussion rhythms for younger children to copy.

32